Tʜ
THE CROSS
Sᴛ. Jᴏsᴇᴍᴀʀíᴀ Esᴄʀɪᴠá

OPENING PRAYER

My Lord and my God,
under the loving eyes of our Mother,
we are making ready to accompany you
along this path of sorrow,
which was the price for our redemption.
We wish to suffer all that You suffered,
to offer you our poor, contrite hearts,
because you are innocent, and yet
you are going to die for us,
who are the only really guilty ones.
My Mother, Virgin of sorrows,
help me to relive those bitter hours
which your Son wished to spend on earth,
so that we, who were made from a handful of clay,
may finally live
in libertatem gloriae filiorum Dei,
in the freedom and glory of the children of God.

FIRST STATION
JESUS IS CONDEMNED TO DEATH

V. We adore you,
O Christ, and
we bless you.

R. Because by your
Holy Cross you have
redeemed the world.

It is after ten in the morning. The trial is moving to its close. There has been no conclusive evidence. The judge knows that his enemies have handed Jesus over to him out of envy, and he tries an absurd move: a choice between Barabbas, a criminal accused of robbery and murder, and Jesus, who says he is Christ. The people choose Barabbas, and Pilate exclaims:

What am I to do then, with Jesus? (Mt 27:22).

They all reply: *Crucify him!*

The judge insists: *Why, what evil has he done?*

Once again they respond, shouting: *Crucify him! Crucify him!*

Pilate is frightened by the growing uproar. So he sends for water, and washes his hands in the sight of the people, saying as he does so:

I am innocent of the blood of this just man; it is your affair (Mt 27:24).

And having had Jesus scourged, he hands him over to them to be crucified. Their frenzied and possessed throats fall silent. As if God had already been vanquished.

Jesus is all alone. Far off now are the days when the words of the Man-God brought light and hope to men's hearts, those long processions of sick people whom he healed, the triumphant acclaim of Jerusalem when the Lord arrived, riding on a gentle donkey. If only men had wanted to give a different outlet to God's love! If only you and I had recognized the day of the Lord!

Our Father …	*V.* Have mercy on us, O Lord.
Hail Mary …	*R.* Have mercy on us.

V. We adore you,
O Christ, and
we bless you.

R. Because by your
Holy Cross you have
redeemed the world.

Outside the city, to the northwest of Jerusalem, there is a little hill: Golgotha is its name in Aramaic; *locus Calvariae*, in Latin: the place of skulls or Calvary.

Offering no resistance, Jesus gives himself up to the execution of the sentence. He is to be spared nothing, and upon his shoulders falls the weight of the ignominious cross. But, through love, the Cross is to become the throne from which he reigns.

The people of Jerusalem and those from abroad who have come for the Passover push their way through the city streets, to catch a passing glimpse of Jesus of Nazareth, the King of the Jews. There is a tumult of voices, and, now and then, short silences: perhaps when Jesus fixes his eyes on someone:

If anyone wishes to come after me, let him take up his cross daily and follow me (Lk 9:23).

How lovingly Jesus embraces the wood which is to bring him to death!

Is it not true that as soon as you cease to be afraid of the Cross, of what people call the cross, when you set your will to accept the Will of God, then you find happiness, and all your worries, all your sufferings, physical or moral, pass away?

Truly the Cross of Jesus is gentle and lovable. There, sorrows cease to count; there is only the joy of knowing that we are co-redeemers with Him.

| Our Father … | *V.* Have mercy on us, O Lord. |
| Hail Mary … | *R.* Have mercy on us. |

V. We adore you,
O Christ, and
we bless you.

R. Because by your
Holy Cross you have
redeemed the world.

The heavy Cross cuts and tears into Our Lord's shoulders.

The crowd has swollen into a multitude, and the legionaries can scarcely contain the angry, surging mob which, like a river that has burst its banks, flows through the streets and alleyways of Jerusalem.

The worn out body of Jesus staggers now beneath the huge Cross. His most loving Heart can barely summon up another breath of life for his poor wounded limbs.

To his right and left, Our Lord sees the multitude moving around like sheep without a shepherd. He could call them one by one by their names, by our names. There they are, those who were fed at the multiplication of the loaves and fishes, those who were cured of their ailments, those he taught by the lakeside, on the mountain and in the porticoes of the Temple.

A sharp pain pierces the soul of Jesus; Our Lord falls to the ground exhausted.

You and I can say nothing: now we know why the Cross of Jesus weighs so much. We weep over our wretched failings and also for the terrible ingratitude of the human heart. From the depths of our soul there comes an act of real contrition, that lifts us up from the prostration of sin. Jesus has fallen that we might get up again, each and every time.

Our Father …   *V.* Have mercy on us, O Lord.
Hail Mary …   *R.* Have mercy on us.

FOURTH STATION
JESUS MEETS HIS BLESSED MOTHER

V. We adore you,
O Christ, and
we bless you.

R. Because by your
Holy Cross you have
redeemed the world.

No sooner has Jesus risen from his first fall than he meets his Blessed Mother, standing by the wayside where He is passing.

With immense love Mary looks at Jesus, and Jesus at his Mother. Their eyes meet, and each heart pours into the other its own deep sorrow. Mary's soul is steeped in bitter grief, the grief of Jesus Christ.

O all you that pass by the way, look and see, was there ever a sorrow to compare with my sorrow! (Lam 1:12).

But no one notices, no one pays attention; only Jesus.

Simeon's prophecy has been fulfilled: *thy own soul a sword shall pierce* (Lk 2:35).

In the dark loneliness of the Passion, Our Lady offers her Son a comforting balm of tenderness, of union, of faithfulness; a 'yes' to the divine will.

Hand in hand with Mary, you and I also want to console Jesus, by accepting always and in everything the Will of his Father, of our Father.

Only thus will we taste the sweetness of Christ's Cross, and come to embrace it with all the strength of Love, carrying it in triumph along the ways of the earth.

Our Father …   *V.* Have mercy on us, O Lord.
Hail Mary …   *R.* Have mercy on us.

FIFTH STATION
SIMON OF CYRENE HELPS JESUS TO CARRY THE CROSS

V. We adore you,
O Christ, and
we bless you.

R. Because by your
Holy Cross you have
redeemed the world.

Jesus is exhausted. His footsteps become more and more unsteady, and the soldiers are in a hurry to be finished. So, when they are going out of the city through the Judgment Gate, they take hold of a man who was coming in from a farm, a man called Simon of Cyrene, the father of Alexander and Rufus, and they force him to carry the Cross of Jesus (cf. Mk 15:21).

In the whole context of the Passion, this help does not add up to very much. But for Jesus, a smile, a word, a gesture, a little bit of love is enough for him to pour out his grace bountifully on the soul of his friend. Years later, Simon's sons, Christians by then, will be known and held in high esteem among their brothers in the faith. And it all started with this unexpected meeting with the Cross.

I went to those who were not looking for me; I was found by those that sought me not (Is 65:1).

At times the Cross appears without our looking for it: it is Christ who is seeking us out. And if by chance, before this unexpected Cross which, perhaps, is therefore more difficult to understand, your heart were to show repugnance... don't give it consolations. And, filled with a noble compassion, when it asks for them, say to it slowly, as one speaking in confidence: 'Heart: heart on the Cross! Heart on the Cross!'

Our Father ...   *V.* Have mercy on us, O Lord.
Hail Mary ...   *R.* Have mercy on us.

V. We adore you, O Christ, and we bless you.

R. Because by your Holy Cross you have redeemed the world.

There is no beauty in him, nor comeliness: and we have seen him, and there was no sightliness, that we should be attracted to him. Despised and the most abject of men, a man of sorrows and acquainted with infirmity; and his look was as it were hidden and despised. Whereupon we esteemed him not (Is 53:2-3).

And it is the Son of God who is passing by, a madman... madly in Love!

A woman, Veronica by name, makes her way through the crowd, with a white linen cloth folded in her hands, and with this she reverently wipes the face of Jesus. Our Lord leaves the impression of his Holy Face on the three parts of that veil.

The beloved face of Jesus, that had smiled upon children and was transfigured with glory on Mount Thabor, is now, as it were, concealed by suffering. But this suffering is our purification; the sweat and the blood, which disfigure and tarnish his features, serve to cleanse us.

Lord, help me decide to tear off, through penance, this pitiful mask I have fashioned with my wretched doings... Then, and only then, by following the path of contemplation and atonement, will my life begin to copy faithfully the features of your life. We will find ourselves becoming more and more like You.

We will be other Christs, Christ himself, *ipse Christus.*

Our Father ...   *V.* Have mercy on us, O Lord.
Hail Mary ...   *R.* Have mercy on us.

V. We adore you,
O Christ, and
we bless you.

R. Because by your
Holy Cross you have
redeemed the world.

Outside the walls of the city, the body of Jesus again gives way through weakness, and he falls a second time, amid the shouts of the crowd and the rough handling of the soldiers.

Infirmity of body and bitterness of soul have caused Jesus to fall again. All the sins of men – mine too – weigh down on his Sacred Humanity.

He has borne our infirmities and carried our sorrows, and we have taken him for a leper, and as one struck by God and afflicted. But he was wounded for our iniquities and bruised for our sins. On him fell the punishment that brought us salvation, and by his wounds we have been healed (Is 53:4-5).

Jesus stumbles, but his fall lifts us up, his death brings us back to life.

To our falling again and again into evil, Jesus responds with his determination to redeem us, with an abundance of forgiveness. And, so that no one may despair, again he wearily raises himself, embracing the Cross.

May our stumbles and defeats separate us from Him no more. Just as a feeble child throws itself contritely into the strong arms of its father, you and I will hold tightly to the yoke of Jesus. Only a contrition and humility like this can transform our human weakness into the fortitude of God.

Our Father …	*V.* Have mercy on us, O Lord.
Hail Mary …	*R.* Have mercy on us.

V. We adore you, O Christ, and we bless you.

R. Because by your Holy Cross you have redeemed the world.

Among the people watching Our Lord as he passes by are a number of women who are unable to restrain their compassion and break into tears, perhaps recalling those glorious days spent with Jesus, when everyone exclaimed in amazement: *bene omnia fecit* (Mk 7:37), he has done all things well.

But Our Lord wishes to channel their weeping towards a more supernatural motive, and he invites them to weep for sins, which are the cause of the Passion and which will draw down the rigor of divine justice:

Daughters of Jerusalem, weep not for me, but weep for your-selves and for your children... For if they do these things to the green wood, what shall be done to the dry? (Lk 23:28,31).

Your sins, my sins, the sins of all men, rise up. All the evil we have done and the good that we have neglected to do. The desolate panorama of the countless crimes and iniquities which we would have committed, if He, Jesus, had not strengthened us with the light of his most loving glance.

How little a life is for making atonement!

| Our Father ... | *V.* Have mercy on us, O Lord. |
| Hail Mary ... | *R.* Have mercy on us. |

V. We adore you,
O Christ, and
we bless you.

R. Because by your
Holy Cross you have
redeemed the world.

Our Lord falls for the third time, on the slope leading up to Calvary, with only forty or fifty paces between him and the summit. Jesus can no longer stay on his feet: his strength has failed him, and he lies on the ground in utter exhaustion.

He offered himself up because it was his will; abused and ill-treated, he opened not his mouth, as a sheep led to the slaughter, dumb as a lamb before its shearers (Is 53:7).

Everyone against Him... the people of the city and those from abroad, and the Pharisees and the soldiers and the chief priests... All of them executioners. His Mother – my Mother – weeps.

Jesus fulfills the will of his Father! Poor: naked. Generous: what is there left for him to surrender? *Dilexit me, et tradidit semetipsum pro me* (Gal 2:20), he loved me and delivered himself up unto death for me.

My God! may I hate sin, and unite myself to You, taking the Holy Cross into my arms, so that I, in my turn, may fulfill your most lovable Will... stripped of every earthly attachment, with no other goal but your glory... generously, not keeping anything back, offering myself with you in a perfect holocaust.

Our Father ...	*V.* Have mercy on us, O Lord.
Hail Mary ...	*R.* Have mercy on us.

TENTH STATION
JESUS IS STRIPPED OF HIS GARMENTS

V. We adore you,
O Christ, and
we bless you.

R. Because by your
Holy Cross you have
redeemed the world.

When Our Lord arrives at Calvary, he is given some wine to drink mixed with gall, as a narcotic to lessen in some way the pain of the crucifixion. But Jesus, after tasting it to show his gratitude for that kind service, has not wanted to drink (cf. Mt 27:34). He gives himself up to death with the full freedom of Love.

Then, the soldiers strip Christ of his garments.

From the soles of his feet to the top of his head, there is nothing healthy in him: wounds and bruises and swelling sores. They are not bound up, nor dressed, nor anointed with oil (Is 1:6).

The executioners take his garments and divide them into four parts. But the cloak is without seam, so they say:

It would be better not to tear it, but let us cast lots for it to see whose it shall be (Jn 19:24).

Thus, Scripture is again fulfilled: *They divided my garments among them, and upon my vesture they cast lots* (Ps 21:19).

Despoiled, stripped, left in the most absolute poverty. Our Lord is left with nothing, save the wood of the Cross.

For us to reach God, Christ is the way; but Christ is on the Cross, and to climb up to the Cross we must have our heart free, not tied to earthly things.

Our Father …	*V.* Have mercy on us, O Lord.
Hail Mary …	*R.* Have mercy on us.

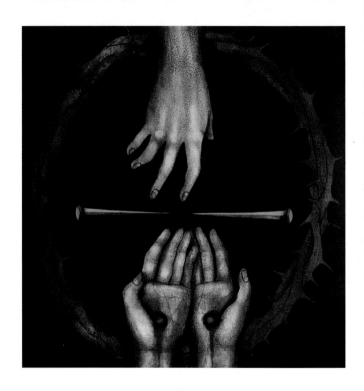

V. We adore you,
O Christ, and
we bless you.

R. Because by your
Holy Cross you have
redeemed the world.

Now they are crucifying Our Lord, and with him two thieves, one on his right and one on his left. Meanwhile, Jesus says:

Father, forgive them for they do not know what they are doing (Lk 23:34).

It is Love that has brought Jesus to Calvary. And once on the Cross, all his gestures and all his words are of love, a love both calm and strong.

With a gesture befitting an Eternal Priest, without father or mother, without lineage (cf. Heb 7:3), he opens his arms to the whole human race.

With the hammerblows with which Jesus is being nailed, there resound the prophetic words of Holy Scripture: *They have pierced my hands and feet. I can count all my bones, and they stare and gloat over me* (Ps 21:17-18).

My people, what have I done to thee, or in what have I saddened thee? Answer me! (Mic 6:3).

And we, our soul rent with sorrow, say to Jesus in all sincerity: I am yours and I give my whole self to You; gladly do I nail myself to the Cross, ready to be in the crossroads of this world a soul dedicated to You, to your glory, to the work of Redemption, the co-redemption of the whole human race.

Our Father ...   *V.* Have mercy on us, O Lord.
Hail Mary ...   *R.* Have mercy on us.

V. We adore you,
O Christ, and
we bless you.

R. Because by your
Holy Cross you have
redeemed the world.

On the uppermost part of the Cross the reason for the sentence is written: *Jesus of Nazareth King of the Jews* (Jn 19:19). And all who pass by insult him and jeer at him. *If he is the king of Israel, let him come down here and now from the cross* (Mt 27:42).

One of the thieves comes to his defence: *This man has done no evil...* (Lk 23:41). Then, turning to Jesus, he makes a humble request, full of faith: *Lord, remember me when thou comest into thy kingdom* (Lk 23:42).

Truly, I say to thee: This day thou shalt be with me in Paradise (Lk 23:43).

At the foot of the Cross stands his Mother, Mary, with other holy women. Jesus looks at her; then he looks at the disciple whom he loves, and he says to his Mother: *Woman, behold thy son.* Then he says to the disciple: *Behold thy mother* (Jn 19:26-27). The sun's light is extinguished and the earth is left in darkness. It is close on three o'clock, when Jesus cries out: *Eli, Eli, lamma sabacthani?* That is: *My God, my God, why hast thou forsaken me?* (Mt 27:46).

Then, knowing that all things are about to be accomplished, that the Scriptures may be fulfilled, he says: *I am thirsty* (Jn 19:28). The soldiers soak a sponge in vinegar and, placing it on a reed of hyssop, they put it to his mouth. Jesus sips the vinegar, and exclaims: *It is accomplished* (Jn 19:30).

The veil of the temple is rent, and the earth trembles, when the Lord cries out in a loud voice: *Father, into thy hands I commend my spirit* (Lk 23:46). And he expires.

Love sacrifice; it is a fountain of interior life. Love the Cross, which is an altar of sacrifice. Love pain, until you drink, as Christ did, the very dregs of the chalice.

Our Father ...	*V.* Have mercy on us, O Lord.
Hail Mary ...	*R.* Have mercy on us.

V. We adore you, O Christ, and we bless you.

R. Because by your Holy Cross you have redeemed the world.

Mary stands by the Cross, engulfed in grief. And John is beside her. But it is getting late, and the Jews press for Our Lord to be removed from there.

Having obtained from Pilate the permission required by Roman law for the burial of condemned prisoners, there comes to Calvary *a councillor named Joseph, a good and upright man, a native of Arimathea. He has not consented to their counsel and their doings, but is himself one of those waiting for the kingdom of God* (Lk 23:50-51). With him too comes Nicodemus, *the same who earlier visited Jesus by night; he brings with him a mixture of myrrh and aloes, about a hundred pounds weight* (Jn 19:39).

These men were not known publicly as disciples of the Master. They had not been present at the great miracles, nor did they accompany him on his triumphal entry into Jerusalem. But now, when things have turned bad, when the others have fled, they are not afraid to stand up for their Lord.

Between the two of them they take down the body of Jesus and place it in the arms of his most holy Mother. Mary's grief is renewed.

Where has thy Beloved gone, o fairest of women? Where has he whom thou lovest gone, and we will seek him with thee? (Song 5:17).

The Blessed Virgin is our Mother, and we do not wish to, we cannot, leave her alone.

Our Father ...	*V.* Have mercy on us, O Lord.
Hail Mary ...	*R.* Have mercy on us.

FOURTEENTH STATION
JESUS IS LAID IN THE TOMB

V. We adore you,
O Christ, and
we bless you.

R. Because by your
Holy Cross you have
redeemed the world.

Very near Calvary, in an orchard, Joseph of Arimathea had had a new tomb made, cut out of the rock. Since it is the eve of the solemn Pasch of the Jews, Jesus is laid there. Then Joseph, *rolling a great stone, closes the grave door and goes away* (Mt 27:60).

Jesus came into the world with nothing; so too, with nothing – not even the place where he rests – he has left us.

The Mother of Our Lord – my Mother – and the women who have followed the Master from Galilee, after taking careful note of everything, also take their leave. Night falls.

Now it is all over. The work of our Redemption has been accomplished. We are now children of God, because Jesus has died for us and his death has ransomed us.

Empti enim estis pretio magno! (1 Cor 6:20), you and I have been bought at a great price.

We must bring into our life, to make them our own, the life and death of Christ. We must die through mortification and penance, so that Christ may live in us through Love. And then follow in the footsteps of Christ, with a zeal to co-redeem all mankind.

We must give our life for others. That is the only way to live the life of Jesus Christ and to become one and the same thing with Him.

Our Father …　　*V.* Have mercy on us, O Lord.
Hail Mary …　　*R.* Have mercy on us.

OTHER PUBLISHED WORKS BY
ST. JOSEMARÍA ESCRIVÁ

THE WAY

Beloved by millions, this book is St. Josemaría's spiritually rich collection of points for meditation and prayer. Genial but pointed, THE WAY is born out of deep Christian experience and aims at encouraging people to love God and live for Him. The 999 points which make up THE WAY were written with yearnings to see Christ, the light of the world. Anyone who reads it with the same yearnings will not have opened this book in vain. St. Josemaría Escrivá "has written something more than a masterpiece: he has written straight from the heart, and straight to the heart go the short paragraphs which, like a string of pearls broken but yet complete, make up THE WAY (*L'Osservatore Romano*).

FURROW

Like THE WAY, FURROW is the fruit of St. Josemaría's rich interior life and extensive experience as a pastor. Aphoristic and perfect for meditation, FURROW was written to encourage and ease personal prayer. These 1000 points for spiritual reflection are directed toward the whole human person: body and soul, nature and grace. With the skillful hand of an experienced and holy priest, St. Josemaría interweaves the divine and human and helps one to see how to bring them into harmony in one's own life.

THE FORGE

This is the third collection of St. Josemaría's refreshingly brief but profoundly weighty reflections and meditations on how to live the Christian life to its fullest. Like THE WAY and FURROW, it gives you practical and pointed material for meditation that will help you take your spiritual responsibilities more seriously and move ever closer to the all consuming forge of God's love. St. Josemaría wrote these 1,055 aphorisms, observations, and exhortations to enkindle a desire for holiness and apostolate.

HOLY ROSARY

To say the Holy Rosary, says St. Josemaría in this book of meditations on the mysteries of the Rosary, is a continuous act of faith,
hope and love, of adoration and reparation. He reveals the secret
to overcome monotony and routine when praying the rosary, and
portrays each Mystery with illuminating eyes of faith, helping you
become absorbed in contemplation when you pray to Our Lady.
Although the five Luminous Mysteries were not inaugurated until
after St. Josemaria's death, the meditations based on his writings
were included in an appendix starting in 2003.

CONVERSATIONS WITH
SAINT JOSEMARIA ESCRIVA

This book is a series of press interviews given in the 1960's by
St. Josemaría. They explain what Opus Dei is and describe basic
aspects of its spirit and organization, its aim to spread in all spheres
of society a deep awareness of the universal call to holiness and
apostolate, in the fulfillment of one's ordinary daily work. St. Josemaría also addressed issues on family life, education, society, and
the Church. Freedom of the individual, love for the Church, and
his own supernatural and human warmth are features that perme-
ate CONVERSATIONS.

CHRIST IS PASSING BY

This first published collection of St. Josemaría's homilies is perfect
for individual spiritual reading and meditation. In these homilies
for Advent, Christmas, Lent, Easter, and other highlights of the
Church year, St. Josemaría consistently emphasizes the great truth
that one's most ordinary, human interests can and should reflect
the presence and transcendence of God, and that one should strive
always to sanctify every detail of one's daily life.

FRIENDS OF GOD

This collection of homilies helps one to develop a strong, lasting
friendship with the God who is close to us. Simple, compassion-
ate, and profound, they are a full expression of St. Josemaría's
passionate, expansive love for God. The author gives the reader

a broad picture of the basic human and Christian virtues, so that one can establish and maintain a filial dialogue with God. With a masterful pastor's hand, St. Josemaría combines theological depth with evangelical clarity. He offers not only a lesson in doctrine, but also an introduction to essential aspects of the Christian life.

IN DIALOGUE WITH THE LORD

Originally published in Spanish in 2017 and then in English in 2018, this work contains 25 homilies preached by St. Josemaría between 1967 and 1975. The subjects include identification with Jesus, divine filiation, prayer, interior life, humility, apostolic formation, and fraternal charity.

PASSIONATELY LOVING THE WORLD

A stirring and forceful call by St. Josemaría to seek holiness in the midst of ordinary life and circumstances. First preached outdoors to thousands of benefactors at the University of Navarre, Spain, in October 1967, this homily is now included in both CONVERSATIONS WITH SAINT JOSEMARIA ESCRIVA and IN LOVE WITH THE CHURCH.

IN LOVE WITH THE CHURCH

This book brings together four homilies of St. Josemaría. It offers the reader an opportunity to deepen one's love for the Church and seek to improve one's service to her. St. Josemaría expresses filial love for our Mother the Church in words which are both attractive and compelling.

St. Josemaría Escrivá's works are available at
www.scepterpublishers.org/collections/
st-josemaria-escriva